Novels for Students, Volume 17

Project Editor: David Galens

Editorial: Anne Marie Hacht, Ira Mark Milne, Pam Revitzer, Kathy Sauer, Timothy J. Sisler, Jennifer Smith, Carol Ullmann, Maikue Vang

Research: Nicodemus Ford, Sarah Genik, Tamara Nott

Permissions: Shalice Shah-Caldwell

Manufacturing: Stacy Melson

Imaging and Multimedia: Dean Dauphinais, Leitha Etheridge-Sims, Mary Grimes, Lezlie Light, Luke Rademacher

Product Design: Pamela A. E. Galbreath, Michael Logusz

While every effort has been made to ensure the reliability of the information presented in this publication, The Gale Group, Inc. does not guarantee the accuracy of the data contained herein. The Gale Group, Inc. accepts no payment for listing; and inclusion in the publication of any organization, agency, institution, publication, service, or individual does not imply endorsement of the editors or publisher. Errors brought to the attention of the publisher and verified to the satisfaction of the publisher will be corrected in future editions.

ISBN 0-7876-6029-9
ISSN 1094-3552

Printed in the United States of America
10 9 8 7 6 5 4 3 2 1

Scoop

Evelyn Waugh 1938

Introduction

Evelyn Waugh's *Scoop* (London, 1938) is a satire on journalism. It is based on Waugh's stint as a war correspondent for the London *Daily Mail* in Abyssinia (now Ethiopia) in 1935, during which he covered the war between Abyssinia and Italy. Waugh admitted that he had no aptitude for war reporting, but he did observe closely the activities of his fellow journalists. The result was a satirical, farcical novel that takes lighthearted but deadly aim at the newspaper industry and the journalistic profession.

The plot rests on some comic twists of fortune.

Lord Copper, the arrogant and ignorant owner of the *Daily Beast*, sends out by mistake a naïve writer of nature columns, William Boot, to cover the war in the fictional East African country of Ishmaelia. Geographically, at least, Ishmaelia is identical with Abyssinia. William gets some quick lessons in the devious way of journalists, who are always trying to outwit their colleagues and deliver a scoop. Helped by a series of lucky events, William gets several major scoops himself and returns to London as a world-renowned reporter. But it all means nothing to him, and he is happy to return to his country home, the isolated and dilapidated Boot Magna Hall, where his many eccentric relatives live.

Author Biography

Evelyn Waugh was born on October 28, 1903, in Hampstead, London, England, the son of Arthur

(an editor and publisher) and Catherine Charlotte (Raban) Waugh. He was enrolled at Lancing, a preparatory school, in 1917, where he wrote poetry, edited the school magazine, and was president of the debating society.

Waugh won a scholarship to Hertford College, Oxford, in 1922. At Oxford, he wrote poetry and stories for undergraduate magazines but, because of financial difficulties, he left the university in 1924 without graduating. He enrolled at Heatherley's Art School, and in 1925 he became a secondary school teacher in Wales and then in Buckinghamshire, England.

In 1927, Waugh married Evelyn Gardner. In 1928, his first novel, *Decline and Fall*, appeared. This was a satire on the English upper classes and the English educational system. While Waugh was writing his second novel, *Vile Bodies* (1930), he discovered that his wife was having an affair, so he filed for a divorce.

In 1930, he converted to Roman Catholicism, and he spent much of his time between 1929 and 1937 traveling. He visited the Mediterranean, Ethiopia (then known as Abyssinia), and North Africa, the West Indies and British Guiana, as well as Brazil, Mexico, and the Arctic. He reported on the Italian-Ethiopian war in 1935 and wrote several accounts of his travels, including *Remote People* (1931), about his African journey, and *Waugh in Abyssinia* (1936).

Waugh's third novel, *Black Mischief*, was published in 1932 and cemented his reputation as a brilliant satirist. It was followed by the bleak *A Handful of Dust* (1934), before Waugh returned to lighthearted satire with *Scoop* (1938).

In 1936, the Catholic Church annulled his first marriage, and the following year Waugh married Laura Herbert. This inaugurated a more settled period in his life, although it was interrupted by the outbreak of World War II in 1939. Waugh was given an officer's commission in the Royal Marines; in 1941 he volunteered for service with the No. 8 Commando Forces in the Middle East, and he took part in several raids on the North African coast. In 1944, he joined the British Military Mission to Yugoslavia.

One of Waugh's best-known novels, *Brideshead Revisited*, was published after the war in 1945. It achieved international success, especially in the United States, where it was a Book-of-the-Month Club selection. In 1948, Waugh went on a lecture tour of Catholic universities in the United States.

In the 1950s, Waugh's literary output continued, although the satirist of the 1930s had now developed a deep dislike for contemporary society. His work from this period included the war novels *Men at Arms* (1952) and *Officers and Gentlemen* (1955), an autobiographical novel, *The Ordeal of Gilbert Pinfold* (1957), and a novella, *Love Among the Ruins* (1953). His last novel was another war novel, *Unconditional Surrender* (1961), which was published in the United States as *The End of the Battle*.

Waugh died on April 10, 1966, in Combe Florey, Somerset, England.

Plot Summary

Book 1: The Stitch Service

Scoop begins as the young novelist John Courteney Boot visits his aristocratic friend, Mrs. Julia Stitch, in London. She is in bed, her face covered in a mask of clay while she directs domestic operations. With her are her secretary, her maid, her precocious eight-year-old daughter, and a workman who is painting ruined castles on the ceiling.

Later, Boot explains to Mrs. Stitch as she drives to an appointment that he must leave London because his American girlfriend is driving him crazy. Mrs. Stitch suggests that he go as a war correspondent to Ishmaelia, East Africa, where there is a crisis. She convinces the head of the Megalopolitan Newspaper Corporation, Lord Copper, that Boot is the man to cover the war. But Mr. Salter, the Foreign Editor at the *Daily Beast*, wrongly assumes that the William Boot who writes a nature column for the *Beast* is the man to whom Copper refers.

The countryman Boot lives in the ancient, dilapidated Boot Magna Hall with a crowd of eccentric relatives. William has no desire to leave his home and has never met anyone at the *Beast*. But when he receives a cable from Salter summoning him to London, he assumes it is because of an error in his column the previous week. He goes to London expecting to be fired. The encounter between William and Mr. Salter is uncomfortable for them both. After a series of comic misunderstandings, Salter asks him if he will go to Ishmaelia as a war correspondent. William politely declines, but when Salter tells him that, unless he goes to Ishmaelia, he will be fired, William reluctantly agrees.

The following morning, William meets Lord Copper. Copper wants the war in Ishmaelia to be resolved quickly and in a way that will create good news copy. After the meeting, Salter tries to explain to William who is fighting and why, but William is none the wiser.

After a comical episode in which William visits two rival Ishmaelite legations in London to get a visa, he flies by private plane to Paris, kindly allowing a stranger to fly with him. Then he boards the train for Marseilles, where he meets the stranger again, who turns out to be an Englishman. The stranger promises to repay William's favor whenever he can.

William then has an uncomfortable journey by sea to Aden. He meets an English journalist named Corker, who is also going to Ishmaelia but knows no more about the place than William. Corker explains the fundamentals of journalism to William, including how to interpret cryptic cables he receives from London. In Aden, William meets up again with the mysterious Englishman, and Corker searches for a story for his news agency.

Book 2: Stones £20

The narrator explains the brewing conflict in Ishmaelia, a backward place that is corruptly run by the Jackson family, with General Gollancz Jackson as president. The capital city, Jacksonburg, receives much foreign investment, little of which finds its way to the ordinary people. Six months earlier, trouble began when Smiles Soum, a lowly member of the Jackson family, quarreled with the leadership. He was perceived in London's liberal circles as a fascist, and support poured in for the president. Journalists flocked to the country, as war seemed imminent.

At the Hotel Liberty, a celebrated American journalist, Wenlock Jakes, is working on a book on English political and social life. There are journalists from many countries at the hotel, including the Englishmen Shumble, Whelper, Pigge, Sir Jocelyn Hitchcock, William, and Corker. The journalists are under pressure from their newspapers to cable a story, but little is happening. Eventually, Shumble makes up a story that a Russian spy has arrived disguised as a railway official. The story is treated as a world scoop but is soon killed by a chorus of denials.

William meets an old friend from school, Jack Bannister, at the British Consulate. Bannister tells him that there is, in fact, a Russian agent in Jacksonburg, but they do not know what he is up to. William is elated at getting such a tip-off, but Corker tells him it will not work after all the previous denials about the presence of a Russian agent.

More journalists arrive, and William moves to the Pension Dressler, run by a formidable German woman, Frau Dressler. There he meets Kätchen, a young German woman who is temporarily separated from her husband. They strike up a friendship, and she persuades him to buy her husband's collection of stones, which he later finds out is gold ore.

Media Adaptations

- An unabridged audiocassette tape of *Scoop*, narrated by Simon Cadell, is published by Cover to Cover Cassettes Ltd. (1998).

The journalists fall to quarreling amongst themselves, and then they all go on a trek to a place called Laku, where they have been led to believe there is some action. Laku, in fact, does not exist.

William receives instructions from his newspaper to remain in Jacksonburg. He is now the only correspondent left there, but he fails to send any news stories. The *Beast* office in London gets increasingly impatient with him and sends him a cable telling him he has been fired. Meanwhile, William has fallen in love with Kätchen. Kätchen persuades him to pay her to get news for him, since she knows some important people. She later informs him that the president has been locked up in his own palace, and William sends a cable with his first news item. The delighted *Beast* reinstates him.

At the British Legation, Bannister explains the political situation to William. He reveals that the Germans are backing the rebellion of Smiles, but the Russians are supporting the communist Young Ishmaelite Party. There is likely to be a communist-inspired coup, followed by a dictatorship. This is another scoop for William.

Kätchen's husband returns, as does Kätchen, who has been imprisoned because her papers were not in order. William is full of regret at losing her, but he cooperates in an escape plan. The two Germans escape down the river by using a canoe that William brought with him in his luggage.

When William returns from seeing them off, he discovers that the Young Ishmaelite Party has taken over the government, the Jacksons have been imprisoned, and a Soviet state has been declared.

As William despairs over his loss of Kätchen,

the mysterious Englishman reappears, by parachute. He likes to be called Mr. Baldwin, and it turns out that he is a savvy businessman who has a large financial interest in Ishmaelia and has been manipulating events to his advantage. He explains the political situation, giving William yet another scoop, and then arranges a quick counterrevolution that topples the day-old Soviet state. President Jackson is reinstated. Mr. Baldwin then writes William's story for him and cables it to the *Beast*.

Book 3: Banquet

[handwritten: lift on William's plane → met on train → predicted would reform favour = Now !!]

Back in London, Lord Copper recommends William to the prime minister for a knighthood. But by mistake the letter informing him of this is delivered to John Courteney Boot, the novelist.

William returns to England, covered in glory because of his journalistic successes. Other newspapers woo his services, and literary agents want his autobiography. But William wants only to return to his home at Boot Magna, from where he writes to Lord Copper declining his invitation to a banquet. Mr. Salter is sent to Boot Magna to bring William back, but he has a very uncomfortable time in the country and cannot persuade William to attend the banquet. The situation is saved when William's uncle Theodore shows up in the offices of the *Beast*, and it is agreed that he will be passed off as William Boot. At the banquet, Lord Copper goes along with the deception. Back at Boot Magna, William is free to continue writing his nature columns, which is all he ever wanted to do.

Mr. Baldwin

Mr. Baldwin is a small, mysterious man who, with his servant, joins William on his flight to Paris. He also turns up on the train to Marseilles. Later in the novel, he parachutes in to Jacksonburg and explains to William the political maneuverings going on in the country. It appears that Baldwin, which is simply the name he prefers to be known by, is a well-connected international businessman who is out to profit personally from the turbulent situation in Ishmaelia, whilst also preserving British economic interests. He owns the mineral rights in Ishmaelia, rights that the Russian and German governments are scheming to acquire. Eventually, it is Mr. Baldwin who writes the text of the final news story that William sends to the *Beast*. In that story, Baldwin refers to himself as a "mystery financier" and compares himself favorably to two of the great Englishmen of the past, Lawrence of Arabia and Cecil Rhodes, founder of Rhodesia (now Zimbabwe). Baldwin also arranges the counterrevolution that topples the day-old Soviet state in Ishmaelia. Abyssinia / Ethiopia

Jack Bannister

Jack Bannister is a senior official in the British Legation in Ishmaelia. He is an old school friend of

William Boot and passes on to him vital information about the country's political situation.

Doctor Benito

Doctor Benito is a rather sinister figure who is the Minister of Foreign Affairs and Propaganda in Ishmaelia. The journalist Pigge regards him as "creepy." Small and neatly dressed, suave and self-possessed, Benito allies himself with the Russianbacked Young Ishmaelite party and, when President Jackson is overthrown, he emerges as the new dictator. But his hold on power lasts only one day; he is toppled by the counterrevolution arranged by Mr. Baldwin.

Uncle Bernard

Uncle Bernard, one of William's uncles, spends his life conducting scholarly research on the family pedigree. Had he had more money, he would have made a claim to the vacant barony of de Butte.

Nanny Bloggs

Nanny Bloggs is William's old nanny at Boot Magna Hall.

John Courteney Boot

John Courteney Boot is a successful writer. He has written eight books, including novels, as well as travel and history books, and he is a well-known and respected name in intellectual circles. He accepts Mrs. Stitch's recommendation to become a war correspondent for the *Daily Beast* because he is desperate to get away from his American girlfriend. But there is a mix-up, and his remote cousin, William Boot, gets the coveted job. At the end of the novel, yet another bureaucratic mix-up ensures that a knighthood intended for William goes instead to John Courteney. Finally, still trying to evade his girlfriend, John Courteney Boot goes off to Antarctica as a reporter for the *Beast*.

Priscilla Boot

Priscilla Boot is William's sister. It is she who, as a joke, inserts all the references in William's article to the fictitious "great crested grebe."

William Boot

William Boot lives in the country at Boot Magna Hall, from where he writes a twice-weekly nature column for the *Daily Beast* called Lush Places. When a misunderstanding occurs, William is sent to Ishmaelia as a war correspondent, but he is a countryman and has little knowledge of the wider world. Even on the train journey to London, he makes a fool of himself, first in the dining-car, ordering whiskey when all they are serving is tea, and then in the carriage when he pays for a drink with an old sovereign, mistaking it for another coin, a shilling. Everyone stares at him.

William is an honest, good-natured man, but he is also very naïve and passive. He has no idea of how to do the job that has been assigned to him. Corker has to teach him the elements of journalism, but even then he shows himself to be an unpromising student, failing to understand the urgency with which he is required to gather news at any cost. Then he foolishly falls in love with the German woman Kätchen and allows her to exploit him for money. It is only through a series of fortuitous events that William gets the scoops that make him famous. When he returns to London, he is unprepared for the glory and renown that now accompanies him, and he turns down all manner of offers from the literary and journalistic world that would have made him rich and even more famous. All he wants is to return home to the peaceful, unchanging world in the country that he knows and loves, and it is his good fortune that another misunderstanding involving the name Boot allows him to do just that.

Lord Copper

Lord Copper is the proprietor of the Megalopolitan Newspaper Corporation. He relishes his position of power and the trappings that go along with it, and he also possesses a grandiose sense of his own importance. This is suggested by the larger-than-life statue of him that stands in the entrance lobby of the Megalopolitan building in London's Fleet Street. Lord Copper claims that he allows his journalists to hold their own opinions, but, in truth, he has very pronounced ideas about the stories he is prepared to print. He is a powerful and ruthless man who likes to have his own way and usually succeeds in getting it. He dominates his staff, none of whom dares to contradict him, which means that Lord Copper is never made aware of the ignorance he displays on many topics. Nor does he realize that he is regarded as a bore, a fact that can be seen by the attitude of his guests at the banquet. The only person who enjoys Lord Copper's regular banquets is Lord Copper himself, largely because they give him the chance to give a long, uninterrupted after-dinner speech.

Corker

Corker is an English journalist whom William first encounters on the train to Marseilles. Gregarious, irreverent, and worldly wise, Corker is the opposite of William. Observing William's ignorance, he takes him under his wing, trying to teach him the basics of journalism. When Corker is pressed by Universal News, his news agency, to send a story, he concocts one based on the flimsiest research.

Frau Dressler

Frau Dressler is a German woman who runs a hotel, the Pension Dressler, which acts as center for the Germans in Jacksonburg. Frau Dressler has lived in Africa all her life. She is a large woman with a lot of energy who drives a hard bargain with the local peasants when they sell her their wares.

Sir Jocelyn Hitchcock

Sir Jocelyn Hitchcock is a famous English journalist who travels to Ishmaelia. He hides out by himself and, because of his reputation, all the other journalists are afraid that he is working on a big story somewhere that they have missed. Hitchcock eventually concocts a fake interview with the leader of the fascists, which supposedly took place in a town called Laku, a place that does not in fact exist. This piece of disinformation sends all the other journalists off on a wild goose chase to Laku, while Sir Jocelyn returns to Europe to work on his next assignment.

Wenlock Jakes

Wenlock Jakes is the highest paid journalist in the United States; his work is syndicated all over America. However, according to Corker, Jakes's methods leave a lot to be desired, since he tends to make his stories up. He even won a Nobel Peace Prize for his courageous reporting of a revolution in the Balkans but, according to Corker, that revolution only began because Jakes's story created such an unstable situation that within a week a revolution actually did occur. Jakes spends his time in Jacksonburg writing a book called *Under the Ermine*, a trashy exposé of English political and social life, for which has been paid a large advance by the publisher.

Kätchen

Kätchen is a young German woman who is temporarily separated from her husband and is staying at the Pension Dressler. Under her helpless exterior, Kätchen is amiably cunning, and she easily gets William, who falls in love with her, to fork over money to her from his expense account. She gets into trouble with the authorities in Ishmaelia because her immigration papers are not in order. As a result, she is briefly imprisoned. Kätchen is naïve in political matters and believes that a solution to her difficulties is to marry William. She thinks this will automatically make her a British citizen, safe from detention. Eventually, she and her returning husband escape down a river in William's canoe.

Erik Olafsen

Erik Olafsen is the resident Jacksonburg correspondent of a syndicate of Scandinavian newspapers. He plays many roles: he is also Swedish vice-consul, a surgeon at the hospital, and the proprietor of the Tea, Bible and Chemist shop. Olafsen is a large man with an eccentric character. He claims that he came to Ishmaelia as a refugee after he killed his grandmother in Sweden. It is Olafsen whom Mr. Baldwin chooses to put the counterrevolution into operation. The drunken Swede single-handedly routs the young Ishmaelite delegates as they listen to Doctor Benito.

Mr. Pappenhacker

Mr. Pappenhacker is the reporter for the communist newspaper *The Twopence*. He is more educated than the other journalists and tends to keep himself apart from them. He also makes a habit of being rude to waiters, since he thinks this will make them dissatisfied with the capitalist system and so hasten the communist revolution.

Pigge

Pigge is one of the English journalists in Ishmaelia.

Uncle Roderick

Uncle Roderick is the least eccentric of William's three uncles. He manages the financial affairs of the family estate and household.

Mr. Salter

Mr. Salter is the foreign editor at the *Daily Beast*. He does not like his hectic job, which he calls a "dog's life," and he knows little about foreign affairs. Nor did he like his previous job as editor of the women's page, which was much too difficult and stressful compared to the only job he really loved—the one at which he was able to choose the jokes in *Clean Fun*, one of Lord Copper's comic weeklies. However, Salter never expresses his discontent to Lord Copper. On the contrary, he is obsequious to his boss and never ventures to correct any of Lord Copper's errors or misstatements.

Mr. Salter lives an ordered, conventional life in London and regards the countryside as hostile territory. His visit to Boot Magna Hall confirms his worst impressions. He is forced to trek six miles across fields in his business suit to get there, and when he finds himself in the strange company of the Boot family, he is completely out of his depth. At the end of the novel, however, he has more luck. Lord Copper makes him become art editor for home knitting, a job he is sure to like.

Shumble

Shumble is one of the English journalists in Ishmaelia. He invents a story that there is a Russian spy in the country disguised as a railway official. At first the story is treated as a scoop, and Shumble is smug and self-satisfied at his success—but then the other journalists unite to kill the story by publicizing vehement official denials.

Algernon Stitch

Algernon Stitch is the husband of Julia Stitch. He is a minister in the British cabinet.

Mrs. Julia Stitch

Mrs. Julia Stitch, wife of Algernon Stitch, is a beautiful, well-connected, society lady. She is always busy with many things, and she specializes in solving the problems of people in her circle. It is Mrs. Stitch who persuades Lord Copper to hire John Courteney Boot as war correspondent. Mrs. Stitch has one notable eccentricity: she owns a small black car and has a habit of driving it on the sidewalk in order to beat the London traffic.

Uncle Theodore

Uncle Theodore is William Boot's eccentric, old-fashioned uncle who makes frequent, disastrous visits to London. When Mr. Salter visits Boot Magna, Theodore regales him with stories that he hopes are suitable for publication in the *Beast*, although Mr. Salter falls asleep and hears none of them. When Salter wakes, he makes the mistake of telling Theodore to contact the features editor of the *Beast*, which gives Theodore another excuse to make a trip to London. Theodore is taken on by the *Daily Beast* and, in the absence of William Boot, is passed off as the famous journalist Boot at the banquet organized by Lord Copper to honor him.

Themes

Journalism and the Truth

Waugh wrote that his main theme was "to expose the pretensions of foreign correspondents ... to be heroes, statesmen and diplomats." In the novel, he pokes fun at the idea that the profession of journalism is characterized by a disinterested search for the truth. On the contrary, the only concern of the journalists is to file a story that will meet with the approval of their bosses at the newspaper. The goal is to keep one step ahead of the competition, which is why the journalists behave in such an unscrupulous manner toward one another. They steal their competitors' cables and lie about anything they think will give them an advantage. For example, they all say they will be leaving for Laku at "tennish" in the morning, but in fact they are all ready to leave at dawn. The talk of leaving later was simply to try to steal a march on the opposition.

Sir Jocelyn Hitchcock appears to be a past master at tricking his rivals. In Jacksonburg, he lies low so that a rumor will start about his "disappearance." This will make his story, that he has conducted an interview with an important political leader in the town of Laku, appear plausible. In fact, Sir Jocelyn could not have done what he claims, since the town of Laku does not exist. But his fabrication serves his purpose not only of getting out of Ishmaelia, a place he does not like (having filed the story, he is free to move on to his next assignment in Europe), but also of deceiving the other reporters.

This incident highlights a point Waugh wishes to emphasize: the question of whether a particular newspaper story is true or not is a secondary consideration, ranking well behind the need to interest readers and scoop the opposition. The famous American reporter Wenlock Jakes is typical in this respect. He won his reputation partly by filing stories that he simply made up. For example, he sent an eyewitness report of the sinking of the *Lusitania* (a passenger ship that was sunk off the coast of Ireland by the Germans in World War I). The only problem with Jakes's story was that he filed it four hours before the ship was hit. Similarly, Sir Jocelyn Hitchcock managed to give day-to-day reports about an earthquake in Messina without ever leaving the comfort of his desk in London. In Ishmaelia, Shumble takes a leaf out of their book by making up his own story about the presence of a Russian spy in disguise. The irony is that Shumble, although he never knows it, comes close to the truth, even though truth is not his main concern. (There really is a Russian agent in Ishmaelia, although it is not the railway official whom Shumble identifies.)

Much of the theme of the deviousness of the journalistic profession is brought out in William's interactions with Corker. When William receives his first cable from the *Beast*, he misinterprets it to mean that he should stay in Aden. Corker knows perfectly well that the cable does not mean this, but he declines to enlighten William. Only when Corker discovers that he and William are not rivals after all —since the *Beast* is accepting Corker's Universal News agency stories as well as William's—does he let William in on the secrets of the cryptic cables they receive.

When Corker is pressured by his agency to file a story about reactions in Ishmaelia to a proposed international police force, Corker's methods are revealing. He asks just one person, Mrs. Earl Russell Jackson, who runs the hotel where he is staying. She completely misunderstands the question, but that does not stop Corker from inventing a story that the women of Ishmaelia are opposed to an interventionist police force.

It is Corker again who sets William straight about how the newspaper business is run. After Shumble's false story about the Russian spy, William suggests that they simply explain that the story was a mistake. But Corker tells him that such behavior would be "unprofessional"; newspapers do not like printing denials, since too many denials might lead the public to mistrust what they read; besides, it makes it look as if the reporters were not doing their job properly. Instead, Corker assures William that all the journalists must now find a Russian spy, whether he exists or not, so they can keep their newspapers abreast of the breaking story (which, of course, is not really a story at all). The way the process works seems to ensure that the real truth is unlikely to come out.

Satire

Satire is literature that diminishes its subject by ridiculing it. A satire can evoke reactions such as amusement, contempt, or scorn. It can be aimed at an individual, a group of people, an institution, or a whole nation. The object of Waugh's satire is the entire newspaper industry, from the proprietor Lord Copper to the editors in Fleet Street and the foreign correspondents in the field.

Topics for Further Study

- In *Scoop*, the *Daily Beast* has a definite editorial position on the war in Ishmaelia. On the World Wide Web, examine the editorial pages of the *New York Times* and the *Wall St. Journal*. What can you tell about each paper's political position from its editorials? When both editorialize on the same issue, what differing positions do they take up, and what does this indicate about their underlying political philosophies? You can also try the same exercise with the *Washington Post* and the *Washington Times*.

- More people today get their news from television rather than from newspapers. What are the advantages and disadvantages of each medium as a source of news?

- Often in fiction, the protagonist grows and changes as a result of the experiences he undergoes. Does this happen to William Boot, or is he just the same at the end of the novel as he was at the beginning? If he has changed, how is he different?

- In recent wars, such as the Persian Gulf War of 1991 and the war in Afghanistan in 2001–2002, the American government has imposed restrictions on American reporters covering the conflict. This was not the case during the Vietnam War. Should the press have unfettered access to war zones and be free to report whatever is happening, or should restrictions be imposed in the cause of national security? Who should decide?

An example of Waugh's method can be seen in the incident Lord Copper relates, in which he and his star reporter Sir Jocelyn Hitchcock quarreled over the date of the Battle of Hastings, as a result of which Hitchcock left the *Beast* for the *Brute*. The Battle of Hastings, when the invading Normans defeated the army of the Anglo-Saxon King Harold, took place in England in 1066. The date 1066 is known by every English schoolchild, but not, apparently, by England's most famous foreign correspondent. The incident suggests that Hitchcock is ignorant beyond imagination, and also implies that this kind of juvenile dispute is the level on which the newspaper business in Fleet Street is conducted. Even the titles of the newspapers, the *Beast* and the *Brute*, are satiric, mocking their pretensions to be the purveyors of news, information, and culture. Mr. Salter, the *Beast's* foreign editor, is almost as ignorant as Copper's view of Hitchcock. He cannot find Reykjavik on a map, nor can anyone else in his office. He is ill read, never having heard of the well-known novelist John Courteney Boot, and neither he nor the *Beast's* managing editor has the knowledge or ability to judge a writer's style, which is why they both think that William Boot's absurd, high-flown effort, "Feather-footed through the plashy fen passes the questing vole" is an example of good style.

Farce

Satire is usually distinguished from farce. Whereas satire may have a serious purpose in exposing vice or folly and pointing the way to something better, farce is comedy pure and simple. It is designed to make people laugh, using unusual situations or improbable events. Farce often makes use of physical humor such as slapstick or horseplay; it may also use practical jokes.

There are many farcical episodes in the novel. One of the funniest is when the aggressive goat at the Pension Dressler finally breaks the rope that fetters her and sends Dr. Benito's pompous emissary, who has just boasted to William that he was a college welterweight boxing champion, sprawling in the garbage.

Other examples of farce are the series of improbable events due to misunderstandings, such as the confusion over the two (and later three) Boots; the entry of Olafsen in a drunken frenzy to end the revolution almost before it has begun; the journalists' trek to a place that doesn't exist; and Salter's calamitous trek over six miles of country to Boot Magna Hall.

Farce is evident in the dialogue, too, as when Salter and William, when they first meet, talk at cross-purposes and so cannot communicate at all. William is expecting to be fired, while Salter has been instructed to offer him a job. To make matters worse, Salter has been given erroneous ideas about suitable topics of conversation when meeting a man from the country.

There is more farce nearer the end of the novel, when Salter is forced to travel to Boot Magna Hall. The Boots not only make the mistake of thinking that he walked the six miles from the railway station out of choice, but they also leap to the conclusion that his disheveled appearance is because of drunkenness. So, during dinner, when all the poor man needs to boost his flagging spirits is a little alcoholic refreshment, they refuse to give him anything other than water.

Historical Context

The Italo-Ethiopian War

The setting and many of the details in the novel (derive) from the historical situation in Abyssinia (now Ethiopia) in 1935 and 1936. Waugh covered the war as a foreign correspondent for the *Daily Mail*.

Italy invaded Ethiopia in October 1935. The pretext was an incident on the border between Ethiopia and Italian Somaliland. The Italians had superior weaponry and captured the capital city, Addis Ababa—Jacksonburg in the novel—in 1936. Italian fascist dictator Benito Mussolini proclaimed Italy's king Victor Emmanuel III emperor of Ethiopia. (In *Scoop*, the name of would-be dictator Dr. Benito is a deliberate reminder of Benito Mussolini.) The League of Nations opposed the Italian intervention but took only ineffective measures to end it. Britain had a stake in the region, but the other great European powers did not (unlike in the novel, where Britain, Germany, and Russia are all involved). The Italo-Ethiopian war, with its evidence that at least one of the totalitarian powers of Europe (the other was Nazi Germany) had imperialistic designs, contributed to the tensions that led up to World War II in 1939.

In *Waugh in Abyssinia* (1936), Waugh reported on his role as a journalist covering the conflict and offered his cautious support of the Italian intervention.

In 1936, civil war broke out in Spain, in which the nationalist, fascist forces of General Franco attempted to overthrow a socialist government. The socialists received much support from leftist intellectuals in England, some of whom, like George Orwell, even went to Spain to fight against Franco. In the Preface to *Scoop*, Waugh pointed out that, in his plot, he tried to combine elements from the Italo-Ethiopian war with some details drawn from the Spanish civil war. The Spanish element can be seen in the playful description of the government of Ishmaelia as "liberal and progressive" and in the names of some of its leaders. General Gollancz Jackson, for example, is intended to remind readers of Victor Gollancz, a left-wing publisher in England. When conflict breaks out, the Ishmaelian rebels are presented, like Franco's forces, as fascists. And the besieged government wins much support in left-wing circles in England: "In a hundred progressive weeklies and Left Study Circles the matter was taken up and the cause of the Jacksons restarted in ideological form." This passage could equally serve as a description of how the left in England rallied to the cause of the Spanish socialists.

Franco's fascists were victorious in 1939.

Foreign Correspondents

The 1930s were the heyday of the glamorous

newspaper foreign correspondent, both in the United States and Britain. In the days before television, these were the men (and, in a few cases, women) who informed the public about the course of events in the trouble spots of the world. In the United States, the foreign correspondent fulfilled an important function because, at the time, the political landscape was dominated by isolationist thinking. As Arthur Schlesinger, Jr. writes of these correspondents, "[T]heir ardent dispatches brought home to Americans the personalities, ambitions, intrigues, and dangers that were putting the planet on the slippery slope into the Second World War."

Among the most famous American correspondents were John Gunther, Vincent Sheean, Raymond Gram Swing, Dorothy Thompson, Edgar Snow, Harold Isaacs, Paul Scott Mowrer, Edgar Ansel Mowrer, and H. R. Knickerbocker. The latter was the model for Wenlock Jakes in *Scoop*. Knickerbocker was a Pulitzer Prize winner who during his career covered nearly every war front in the world, including the Italo-Ethiopian war, which he covered for Hearst International. He and Waugh struck up a cordial relationship there but quarreled over a remark Knickerbocker made and even came to blows over it.

Gunther, who was head of the *Chicago Daily News* bureau in Vienna in the early 1930s, and who was later transferred to London, wrote in his book *Inside U.S.A.* (quoted by Schlesinger) that the 1930s

Compare & Contrast

- **1930s:** Ethiopia (Abyssinia) is invaded by Italy in 1935. The Italians use poison gas, defying the Geneva Protocol that banned such weapons in 1925. The Italian occupation continues until 1941, when British forces liberate the country.

  Today: After rebels topple the socialist government of Ethiopia in 1991, multiparty elections are held in 1995 for the first time ever. In 1998, a border war breaks out with Eritrea, Ethiopia's northern neighbor. It is resolved by a peace treaty in 2000.

- **1930s:** Newspapers and radio are the only means by which people are informed about world events.

  Today: Most people use television rather than newspapers as their main source of news. However, more and more people are turning to the Internet as a news source. Because of the growth of the Internet, the old concept of a single daily edition of a newspaper is changing. The major newspapers, such as the *New York Times* and the *Washington Post*, have websites in which the main stories are updated every few hours.

- **1930s:** Foreign correspondents such

as H. R. Knickerbocker and John Gunther are well known in America for their vigorous and thorough reporting of world events.

Today: Newspaper foreign correspondents are no longer household names to the American or British public. Their place has been taken by television reporters. Reporters such as MSNBC's Ashleigh Banfield make names for themselves by broadcasting from dangerous parts of the globe. Television and newspaper reporters take risks in doing their jobs, and occasionally there is a tragedy. The kidnapping and murder of *Wall St. Journal* reporter Daniel Pearl in 2002, as he pursued a story about terrorism in Pakistan, illustrates the dangers encountered by reporters in unstable regions of the world.

---

were the bubbling, blazing days of American foreign correspondence in Europe.... Most of us traveled steadily, met constantly, exchanged information, caroused, took in each other's washing, and, even when most fiercely competitive, were devoted friends.... We were scavengers, buzzards, out to get the news, no matter whose wings got clipped.

One of the famous British correspondents was F. A. Voigt. In the 1920s and early 1930s, he was Berlin correspondent for the *Manchester Guardian*. His reporting angered the German authorities, and on one occasion in the early 1920s he was kidnapped; a wall around him was sprayed with bullets, but he escaped. Later, Voigt wrote fearlessly about the menace of Hitler's Nazi Party and had to leave Berlin hurriedly for Paris when Hitler came to power in 1933. Even then he continued to write in opposition to Hitler. Voigt's friends and colleagues used to say that he would rather be burned at the stake than be frightened off a story—an attitude that typified the foreign correspondent in the public mind, although such a glamorous view of the profession was not shared by Waugh, as *Scoop* makes abundantly clear.

A Scoop in Ethiopia

During the Italo-Ethiopian war in 1935–1936, there was one of the most famous journalistic scoops of the century. An Englishman named F. W. Rickett, negotiating on behalf of an American oil company, secured a huge oil and mineral concession from the Ethiopian emperor, Haile Selassie. Rickett (who is the original on which the character Mr. Baldwin in the novel is based) gave the information exclusively to three journalists, including Sir Percival Phillips of the *Daily*

Telegraph. (Phillips is the model for Sir Jocelyn Hitchcock in *Scoop.*)

Waugh missed out on the scoop because, like the crowd of journalists in *Scoop*, he had been out of Addis Ababa chasing another story. The *Daily Mail* was not pleased with his performance and cabled him, "Badly left oil concession suggest your return Addis immediately."

Critical Overview

Scoop was well received by critics on publication in 1938, and this confirmed Waugh's reputation as a writer of humorous and effective satire on whatever subject he chose. Everyone agreed that the novel was amusing and entertaining. The anonymous reviewer for the *Times Literary Supplement*, for example, praised Waugh's "ribald wit" that "spurts in a brisk uninterrupted flow upon the caprices of sensational journalism." But the reviewer also found that the character William Boot "is too much the simpleton, too facile an instrument for satire," and he thought it fitting that the knighthood at the end should go to John Boot rather than to William.

Novelist John Brophy, in an appreciative review in the *Daily Telegraph*, commented that Waugh as a writer was extremely good at making people laugh. But this alone did not make him a satirist, "for indignation founded on some belief is necessary to satire, and I have never been able from his books to discover what Mr. Waugh believes in."

In the *Spectator*, Derek Verschoyle declared *Scoop* to be an "enchanting book," admiring the calm way in which Waugh demolishes his satirical targets, without "surprise, sentiment or resentment." Verschoyle picked out the depiction of the Boot family as the highlight of the book: "[it] reveals an inventive power which it is little exaggeration to call that of genius."

Since its positive initial reception, however, *Scoop* has not usually been ranked with the very best of Waugh's achievements. It often takes a back seat to Waugh's earlier satires of the 1930s, especially *Vile Bodies* and *Black Mischief.* However, with the general reader, *Scoop* has been and remains one of Waugh's most popular novels.

What Do I Read Next?

- Waugh's *Brideshead Revisited: The Sacred and Profane Memories of Captain Charles Ryder* (1945) chronicles twenty years in the lives of the Marchmains, a wealthy English Catholic family. Unlike his earlier novels, this is not a satire but an exploration of love, politics, and the call of religion.

- English comic writer P. G. Wodehouse was one of the influences on *Scoop*, and his novel *Full Moon* (1947) is one of his most popular romantic farces. The setting of Blandings Castle is similar to Boot Magna in *Scoop*, and the intricate plotting, eccentric characters, and happy ending make the novel a classic of its kind.

- *Secrets of the Press: Journalists on Journalism* (1999), edited by Stephen Carter, is an entertaining collection of essays by British journalists on the state of the profession today. The essays by Christopher Munnion ("Into Africa"), Ann Leslie ("Female 'Firemen'"), and Emma Daly ("Reporting from the Front") describe, often amusingly, their experiences as foreign correspondents.

- Selina Hastings's *Evelyn Waugh: A Biography* (1994) was written with the full support of Waugh's family, who were dismayed at the negative portrayal of Waugh's personality in an earlier biography by Martin Stannard. Hastings presents a more balanced view that aims to give as close an impression as possible of what it was like to know the man.

Sources

Amsden, David, "Death or Glory: When the stakes are high, British journalist Daniel Jeffreys always gets the story—and he never lets the facts get in the way," in *New York*, May 6, 2002.

Brophy, John, Review of *Scoop*, in *Evelyn Waugh: The Critical Heritage*, edited by Michael Stannard, Routledge & Kegan Paul, 1984, pp. 198–99, originally published in *Daily Telegraph*, May 13, 1938.

Review of *Scoop*, in *Evelyn Waugh: The Critical Heritage*, edited by Michael Stannard, Routledge & Kegan Paul, 1984, pp. 197–98, originally published in *Times Literary Supplement*, May 7, 1938.

Schlesinger, Arthur J., Jr., "A Man from Mars," in *Atlantic Monthly*, Vol. 279, No. 4, April 1997, pp. 113–18.

Stannard, Michael, *Evelyn Waugh: The Early Years, 1903–1939*, J. M. Dent & Sons, 1986.

Teel, Leonard Ray, Foreword, in *Evelyn Waugh in Ethiopia: The Story behind "Scoop,"* by Michael Brian Salwen, Edwin Mellen Press, 2001, p. v.

Verschoyle, Derek, Review of *Scoop*, in *Evelyn Waugh: The Critical Heritage*, edited by Michael Stannard, Routledge & Kegan Paul, 1984, pp. 199–201, originally published in *Spectator*, May 13, 1938.

Waugh, Evelyn, *Scoop*, Little Brown and Co., 1977, pp. 133, 215.

——, *Waugh in Abyssinia*, Longmans, Green and Company, 1936.

Further Reading

Beaty, Frederick L., *The Ironic World of Evelyn Waugh: A Study of Eight Novels*, Northern Illinois University Press, 1992.

> Beaty examines the role that irony plays in Waugh's fiction, in terms of plot, theme, and character. He argues that Waugh's use of irony adds unstated and often crucial meaning to the text.

Crabbe, Kathryn W., *Evelyn Waugh*, Continuum, 1988.

> This is a readable survey of Waugh's novels, but in the chapter on *Scoop*, Crabbe makes the error of confusing the two characters Sir Jocelyn Hitchcock and Wenlock Jakes.

Davis, Robert Murray, *Evelyn Waugh, Writer*, Pilgrim Books, Inc., 1981.

> This includes a chapter on *Scoop*, in which Davis analyzes the changes Waugh made as he revised the novel from early drafts.

Lane, Calvin W., *Evelyn Waugh*, Twayne English Authors Series, No. 301, Twayne Publishers, 1981.

> Lane concentrates on Waugh's fiction, with chapters on all the

major novels. He also discusses Waugh's views on the craft of fiction and offers an evaluation of Waugh's achievement as a satiric novelist.

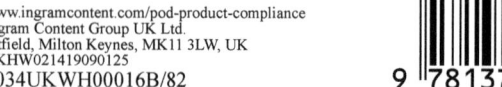